AF582913

BEFORE YOU SAY 'I DO'

Points to Ponder Before Proceeding to the Marriage Altar

Adeniyi Adekunle

BEFORE YOU SAY "I DO":
Points to Ponder Before Proceeding To The Marriage Altar

ISBN: 978 - 978 - 942 - 955 - 4

Published in Nigeria by Silverpen Publishing Hosue
16, Shopeju Street, Ladipo Lagos
Tel: +2347086925800

Many different translations have been used for the purpose of clarity, to help the reader better understand the truths revealed in the scripture. Some of the translations used are:

- New King James Version (NKJV)
- New International Version (NIV)
- Amplified Version (AMP)
- The Living Bible (TLB)
- New Living Translation (NLT)
- The Message (MSG)

a SENSE & CENTURY MEDIA production:
Author's Contacts:
T: +234 805 7200 197
+234 808 785 4854
+234 702 528 7000
E: sandc.tools@gmail.com

Printed in The Federal Republic of Nieria

CoNTENTS

INTRODUCTION

Deciding the person to marry is one of the most important decisions people have to make in life. No other decision impacts directly on your life as much as whom you decide to marry.

Before deciding on whom to marry, the most complicated decision most people have made is deciding the course to study or the school to attend. As important as these decisions are, they do not impact on your life like the decision of whom to marry.

By the time most young people are concluding their tertiary education, or by the time they get their first job, they begin to seriously consider "settling down." They find somebody, "fall in love," and get married, believing they have "settled down." Five years after, they discover they have never been more "unsettled" in their entire life; and since their marriage seems not to be fulfilling their dream of "settling down," it ends up breaking down.

School usually have guidance counsellors that guide students in choosing a course of study. Schools also prepare brochures to help you make informed decisions before committing yourself to enrolling with them. But where are the counsellors that guide you before choosing your course in marriage. Which information brochure did you consult to help you make an informed decision before committing your life to someone in marriage?

In the fields of construction and architecture, designs and models are very essential for the successful completion of buildings and other kinds of structures. These designs and models give a pattern of what the finished product will look like. The home is a far more important structure. When it comes to marriage, God gives us designs and models and expects us to follow them if we are to get His desired outcome. In Hebrews 8:5, God warned Moses as he was embarking on the project of building the tabernacle.

"God gave him this warning: "Be sure that you make everything according to the pattern I have shown you here on the mountain."

Hebrews 8:5b (NLT)

, "Look to Abraham your father, And to Sarah who bore you; For I called him alone, And blessed him and increased him."

Isaiah 51:2 (NKJV)

God is saying, "Do you want a great home like that of Abraham and Sarah? Then model your life after them, and you will experience what they experienced."

God uses model and patterns to teach us. Through Abraham, God gave a model, a pattern that can be used by those who are planning to choose a life partner. The biblical account of how Isaac married Rebekah gives us some insights that are very relevant to us today.

The points that have been gleaned from this biblical account are to serve as a guide, and not as a rule or formula for choosing whom to marry. Abraham's servant said *"...being on the way, the Lord led me..." (Gen 24:27).*

My prayer and desire for you is that as you allow these points to guide you, you will experience the leading of the Lord in a clear and practical way.

This is the account of how Isaac got a wife:

Abraham was now a very old man, and the Lord had blessed him in every way. One day Abraham said to his oldest servant, the man in charge of his household, "Take an oath by putting your hand under my thigh. Swear by the Lord, the God of heaven and earth, that you will not allow my son to marry one of these local Canaanite women. Go instead to my homeland, to my relatives, and find a wife there for my son Isaac." The servant asked, "But what if I can't find a young woman who is willing to travel so far from home? Should I then take Isaac there to live among your relatives in the land you came from?" "No!" Abraham responded. "Be careful never to take my son there. For the Lord, the God of heaven, who took me from my father's house and my native land, solemnly promised to give this land to my descendants. He will send his angel ahead of you, and he will see to it that you find a wife there for my son. If she is unwilling to come back with you, then you are free from this oath of mine. But under no circumstances are you to take my son there." So the servant took an oath by putting his hand under the thigh of his master, Abraham. He swore to follow Abraham's instructions. Then he loaded ten of Abraham's camels with all kinds of expensive gifts from his master, and he traveled to distant Aram-naharaim. There he went to the town where Abraham's brother Nahor had settled. He made the camels kneel beside a well just outside the town. It was evening, and the women were coming out to draw water. "O Lord, God of my master, Abraham," he prayed. "Please give me success today, and show unfailing love to my master, Abraham. See, I am standing here beside this spring, and the young women of the town are coming out to draw water. This is my request. I will ask one of them, 'Please give me a drink from your jug.' If she says, 'Yes, have a drink, and I will water your camels, too!'—let her be the one you have selected as Isaac's wife. This is how I will know that you have shown unfailing love to my master." Before he had finished praying, he saw a young woman named Rebekah coming out with her water jug on her shoulder. She was the daughter of Bethuel, who was the son of Abraham's brother Nahor and his wife, Milcah. Rebekah was very beautiful and old enough to be married, but she was still a virgin. She went down to the spring, filled her jug, and came up again. Running over to her, the servant said, "Please give me a little drink of water from your jug." "Yes, my lord," she answered, "have a drink." And she quickly lowered her jug from her shoulder and gave him a drink. When she had given him a drink, she said, "I'll draw water for your camels, too, until they have had enough to drink." So she quickly emptied her jug into the watering trough and ran back to the well to draw water for all his camels. The servant watched her in silence, wondering whether or not the Lord had given him success in his mission. Then at last, when the camels had finished drinking, he took out a gold ring for her nose and two large gold bracelets for her wrists. "Whose daughter are you?" he asked. "And please tell me, would your father have any room to put us up for the night?" "I am the daughter of Bethuel," she replied. "My grandparents are Nahor and Milcah. Yes, we have plenty of straw and feed for the camels, and we have room for guests." The man bowed low and worshiped the Lord. "Praise the Lord, the God of my master, Abraham," he said. "The Lord has shown unfailing love and faithfulness to my master, for he has led me straight to my master's relatives." The young woman ran home to tell her family everything that had happened. Now Rebekah had a brother named Laban, who ran out to meet the man at the spring. He had seen the nose-ring and the bracelets on his sister's wrists, and had heard Rebekah tell what the man had said. So he rushed out to the spring, where the man was still standing beside his camels. Laban said to him,"Come and stay with us, you who are blessed by the Lord! Why are you standing here outside the town when I have a room all ready for you and a place prepared for the camels?" So the man went home with Laban, and Laban unloaded the camels, gave him straw for their bedding, fed them, and provided water for the man and the camel drivers to wash their feet. Then food was served. But Abraham's servant said, "I don't want to eat until I have told you why I have come." "All right," Laban said, "tell us." "I am Abraham's servant," he explained. "And the Lord has greatly blessed my master; he has become a wealthy man. The Lord has given him flocks of sheep and goats, herds of cattle, a fortune in silver and gold, and many male and female servants and camels and donkeys. "When Sarah, my master's wife, was very old, she gave birth to my master's son, and my master has given him everything he owns. And my master made me take an oath. He said, 'Do not allow my son to marry one of these local Canaanite women. Go instead to my father's house, to my relatives, and find a wife there for my son.' "But I said to my master, 'What if I can't find a young woman who is willing to go back with me?' He responded, 'The Lord, in whose presence I have lived, will send his angel with you and will make your mission successful. Yes, you must find a wife for my son from among my relatives, from my father's family. Then you will have fulfilled your obligation. But if you go to my relatives and they refuse to let her go with you, you will be free from my oath.' "So today when I came to the spring, I prayed this prayer: 'O Lord, God of my master, Abraham, please give me success on this mission. See, I am standing here beside this spring. This is my request. When a young woman comes to draw water, I will say to her, "Please give me a little drink of water from your jug." If she says, "Yes, have a drink, and I will draw water for your camels, too," let her be the one you have selected to be the wife of my master's son.' "Before I had finished praying in my heart, I saw Rebekah coming out with her water jug on her shoulder. She went down to the spring and drew water. So I said to her, 'Please give me a drink.' She quickly lowered her jug from her shoulder and said, 'Yes, have a drink, and I will water your camels, too!' So I drank, and then she watered the camels. "Then I asked, 'Whose daughter are you?' She replied, 'I am the daughter of Bethuel, and my grandparents are Nahor and Milcah.' So I put the ring on her nose, and the bracelets on her wrists. "Then I bowed low and worshiped the Lord. I praised the Lord, the God of my master, Abraham, because he had led me straight to my master's niece to be his son's wife. So tell me—will you or won't you show unfailing love and faithfulness to my master? Please tell me yes or no, and then I'll know what to do next." Then Laban and Bethuel replied, "The Lord has obviously brought you here, so there is nothing we can say. Here is Rebekah; take her and go. Yes, let her be the wife of your master's son, as the Lord has directed." When Abraham's servant heard their answer, he bowed down to the ground and worshiped the Lord. Then he brought out silver and gold jewelry and clothing and presented them to Rebekah. He also gave expensive presents to her brother and mother. Then they ate their meal, and the servant and the men with him stayed there overnight. But early the next morning, Abraham's servant said, "Send me back to my master." "But we want Rebekah to stay with us at least ten days," her brother and mother said. "Then she can go." But he said, "Don't delay me. The Lord has made my mission successful; now send me back so I can return to my master." "Well," they said, "we'll call Rebekah and ask her what she thinks." So they called Rebekah. "Are you willing to go with this man?" they asked her. And she replied, "Yes, I will go." So they said good-bye to Rebekah and sent her away with Abraham's servant and his men. The woman who had been

Rebekah's childhood nurse went along with her. They gave her this blessing as she parted: "Our sister, may you become the mother of many millions! May your descendants be strong and conquer the cities of their enemies." Then Rebekah and her servant girls mounted the camels and followed the man. So Abraham's servant took Rebekah and went on his way. Meanwhile, Isaac, whose home was in the Negev, had returned from Beer-lahai-roi. One evening as he was walking and meditating in the fields, he looked up and saw the camels coming. When Rebekah looked up and saw Isaac, she quickly dismounted from her camel. "Who is that man walking through the fields to meet us?" she asked the servant. And he replied, "It is my master." So Rebekah covered her face with her veil. Then the servant told Isaac everything he had done. And Isaac brought Rebekah into his mother Sarah's tent, and she became his wife. He loved her deeply, and she was a special comfort to him after the death of his mother. Gen 24:1-67

CHAPTER ONE

ARE You REALLY READY FoR MARRIAGE? DECIDE

'One day Abraham said to his oldest servant, the man in charge of his household, "Take an oath by putting your hand under my thigh. Swear by the Lord, the God of heaven and earth, that you will not allow my son to marry one of these local Canaanite women. 4 Go instead to my homeland, to my relatives, and find a wife there for my son Isaac."

Genesis 24:2-4 (NLT)

Every great destiny begins with a decision. Marriage is honourable, but the truth is that marriage is not for everybody. Jesus said:

"There are different reasons why some men cannot marry. Some men were born without the ability to become fathers. Others were made that way later in life by other people. And some men have given up marriage because of the kingdom of heaven. But the person who can marry should accept this teaching about marriage."

Matthew 19:12 (NCV)

Before you even begin to think of what you need to do before you saying 'I do' to anybody, you need to ask yourself "Am I really ready for marriage?" or "Do I want to get married at all?"

These are simple but profound questions because whatever you decide based on your answer to these questions will alter the course of your life forever. I have met people that have no desire to be married; I have met people who desired marriage but wanted it much later in life; and I have also met people who said they were really eager to be married whereas from their actions, it was clear they were not really ready for marriage.

When you are really ready for marriage, you decide; and by deciding, you have taken a position. The position you have taken will be evident in the things you do. The decision to be married is not the only decision you will have to make, but it is a major decision that will be supported by many other decisions.

Before Isaac could get a wife at all, a decision had to be made about the fact that 'Isaac has to be married.' Abraham summoned his chief servant and told him, "I have made a decision; Isaac needs to be married..." After Abraham's decision was made, subsequent decisions now followed. But all the others came after the marriage decision had been made.

So are you really willing to get married?

Don't let anyone force or coerce you into making a decision, the choice is really yours. Yes, people may encourage or discourage you about marriage, people might share their marital experiences with you, and those experiences may be good or bad but be absolutely clear on this: IT IS YOUR CHOICE THAT REALLY MATTERS! Rebekah's decision to marry Isaac was also based on her decision. After Abraham's servant had discussed the marriage proposal with her family, they still gave Rebekah the opportunity to make the final decision.

"Well," they said, "we'll call Rebekah and ask her what she thinks." So they called Rebekah. "Are you willing to go with this man?" they asked her. And she replied, "Yes, I will go." So they said good-bye to Rebekah and sent her away with Abraham's servant and his men. The woman who had been Rebekah's childhood nurse went along with her."

Genesis 24:57-59 (NLT)

Nobody should be forced or pressured into marriage. Marriage is for the matured, and one of the major marks of maturity is the ability to make independent decisions. If for some reasons you find yourself heading into a marriage that you are not ready for, please don't go any further. Take your time, slow down, think it through, and then decide. This IS one major thing you need to do before you say 'I do'

CHAPTER TWO

WITHouT HIM You CAN SuccEED AT NOTHING, NoT EvEN AT CHooSING A LIFE PARTNER

One day Abraham said to his oldest servant, the man in charge of his household, "Take an oath by putting your hand under my thigh.. Swear by the Lord, the God of heaven and earth, that you will not allow my son to marry one of these local Canaanite women. Go instead to my homeland, to my relatives, and find a wife there for my son Isaac."

Genesis 24:2-4 (NLT)

When it was time for Abraham to find a wife for Isaac, he knew without divine guidance, he couldn't get it right. After decades of walking with God, one thing had become clear to Abraham: **WITHOUT GOD'S HELP WE CAN ACCOMPLISH NOTHING SIGNIFICANT**. Abraham learnt this lesson the hard way.

God spoke to him at age 75 that he would have a son; but for some reason Abraham felt the promised son wasn't coming as quick as he and Sarah wanted, so they went ahead to make things happen for themselves. Sarah gave Abraham her maid Hagar to bear him a child on her behalf. Although this must have been a common practice among the people at that time, Abraham and Sarah forgot they were not just like everybody else, that they were God's covenant people.

After decades of walking with God, one thing had become clear to Abraham: WITHOUT GOD'S HELP WE CAN ACCOMPLISH NOTHING SIGNIFICANT.

Hagar eventually had a son for Abraham called Ishmael; but God did not accept Ishmael because he was a product of human effort and not the grace of God. Abraham learnt from that experience never to make any move without God's approval. So, in getting a wife for Isaac, Abraham wanted it to be very clear to his servant that it was a very spiritual assignment.

It is dangerous to try to get a life partner without divine guidance. As men, we are limited in our knowledge; we don't even know what the next minute has in store for us. But God is all knowing, He knows yesterday, today, and tomorrow, and so it is wisdom to seek His assistance in choosing a spouse.

Proverbs 3:5-6 Says, "*Trust in the Lord with all your heart, And lean not on your own understanding; In all your ways acknowledge Him, And He shall direct your paths.* " (NKJV) Don't depend solely on your own sense of judgement. In ALL YOUR WAYS, ACKNOWLEDGE HIM and He will direct your affairs.

I have heard some Christian say "God is no longer involved in choosing wives for men, since Adam had blamed Him for Eve's wrongdoing." The subtle implication of this saying is that man is on his own when it comes to choosing a spouse. The truth is that God never chooses a wife for anybody; he didn't even choose for Adam in the first place. The Scripture says God formed the woman and brought her to the man.

When you go to a boutique to buy clothes, the attendant may bring you different designs to choose from. That the attendant brought the clothes to you doesn't mean the attendant chose the clothes for you. The choice is still ultimately yours.

"Then the rib which the Lord God had taken from man He made into a woman, and He brought her to the man. And Adam said: "This is now bone of my bones And flesh of my flesh; She shall be called Woman, Because she was taken out of Man."

Genesis 2:22-23 (NKJV)

Yes, God brought the woman to man, but Adam's statement after he saw Eve showed that he was pleased with what he saw and based on that he made his choice. God still doesn't chose for man; He simply guides us when we seek His help.

Proverbs 19:14 SAYS, *"House and riches are the inheritance from fathers, but a wise, understanding, and prudent wife is from the Lord. "*(AMP)

This Scripture shows clearly that we are not on our own when it comes to choosing a spouse. God desires to help us get a prudent and understanding spouse, but we must consciously acknowledge Him and seek His help.

When Abraham's servant was on his way to find a wife for Isaac, he still prayed saying, *"O Lord, God of my master, Abraham," he prayed. "Please give me success today, and show unfailing love to my master, Abraham."* **Genesis 24:12** (NLT)

For Abraham and members of his household, it was inconceivable to embark on such an assignment without clearly depending on heaven's help. A marriage relationship is the most important relationship between a man and a woman. If you call Jesus your Lord, why should your Lord not have a say when you are going into such a serious relationship.

I know that sometimes, our emotions or body chemistry could override our sense of spiritual perception, especially when we say we are in love. However, committing yourself to a lifelong marital relationship based only on strong emotional chemistry may land you in casualty.

Amnon, King David's son, thought he was in love, when in reality, it was his emotion and his body chemistry that were out or order. The moment the chemistry was satisfied, the so-called love that had made him sick vanished and was replaced by deep hatred.

> *"Now David's son Absalom had a beautiful sister named Tamar. And Amnon, her half brother, fell desperately in love with her. mnon became so obsessed with Tamar that he became ill. She was a virgin, and Amnon thought he could never have her. ut Amnon had a very crafty friend—his cousin Jonadab. He was the son of David's brother Shimea. One day Jonadab said to Amnon, "What's the trouble? Why should the son of a king look so dejected morning after morning?" So Amnon told him, "I am in love with Tamar, my brother Absalom's sister." "Well," Jonadab said, "I'll tell you what to do. Go back to bed and pretend you are ill. When your father comes to see you, ask him to let Tamar come and prepare some food for you. Tell him you'll feel better if she prepares it as you watch and feeds you with her own hands." So Amnon lay down and pretended to be sick. And when the king came*

to see him, Amnon asked him, "Please let my sister Tamar come and cook my favorite dish as I watch. Then I can eat it from her own hands." So David agreed and sent Tamar to Amnon's house to prepare some food for him. When Tamar arrived at Amnon's house, she went to the place where he was lying down so he could watch her mix some dough. Then she baked his favorite dish for him.
9 *But when she set the serving tray before him, he refused to eat. "Everyone get out of here," Amnon told his servants. So they all left. Then he said to Tamar, "Now bring the food into my bedroom and feed it to me here." So Tamar took his favorite dish to him. But as she was feeding him, he grabbed her and demanded, "Come to bed with me, my darling sister." "No, my brother!" she cried. "Don't be foolish! Don't do this to me! Such wicked things aren't done in Israel. Where could I go in my shame? And you would be called one of the greatest fools in Israel. Please, just speak to the king about it, and he will let you marry me." But Amnon wouldn't listen to her, and since he was stronger than she was, he raped her. Then suddenly Amnon's love turned to hate, and he hated her even more than he had loved her. "Get out of here!" he snarled at her.*

2 Samuel 13:1-15 (NLT)

Unfortunately this is the case with some married people today; they are living with their enemy. The fairy tale love affair they thought they had, and upon which they built their marriage is now history, and their home has become a house of horror.

Jesus said, *"...for without Me you can do nothing."* { **John 15:5** (NKJV) } Be sure you have God's guidance before you commit to a marriage relationship.

This one thing you must do before you say 'I do.'

CHAPTER THREE

STAY WITHIN THE FAMILY cHooSE FRoM YouR TRIBE

"Swear by the Lord, the God of heaven and earth, that you will not allow my son to marry one of these local Canaanite women. Go instead to my homeland, to my relatives, and find a wife there for my son Isaac."

Genesis 24:3-4 (NLT)

From time to time, I have some Christians ask me why they have to marry a Christian. They ask why a believer must marry another believer. They say if they can't get a believer to marry, why can't they marry the unbelievers that come their way. Some even go as far as saying that marrying a fellow believer is not a guarantee of having a good marriage and that there are a number of unbelievers that have better marriages than some believers. To be honest, these people actually have a point.

Marriage is such a sensitive relationship that you want to enter into it the right way. Marriage never leaves you the same, and it tests almost everything about you;

because of this, common sense requires that you tread softly and stay with what is familiar.

For Abraham, it was of utmost importance that his son chose a wife from his home country, not from among the Canaanites with whom they lived. Although he lived among the Canaanites, his culture and values were not the same as the Canaanites.

A great life, family or society is built on great values. Abraham had seen the values of the people among whom he lived, and he was sure it was different and dangerous for the future of what God had showed him. The values of his father's house were slightly more acceptable to him. He went on further to warn his servant:

> *"The servant asked, "But what if I can't find a young woman who is willing to travel so far from home? Should I then take Isaac there to live among your relatives in the land you came from?" "No!" Abraham responded. "Be careful never to take my son there. For the Lord, the God of heaven, who took me from my father's house and my native land, solemnly promised to give this land to my descendants. He will send his angel ahead of you, and he will see to it that you find a wife there for my son. If she is unwilling to come back with you, then you are free from this oath of mine. But under no circumstances are you to take my son there."*

Genesis 24:5-8 (NLT)

Abraham was very conscious of the fact that when people don't share similar values, there was bound to be trouble. No wonders, he was willing to take all the trouble of sending his servant to travel so far just to get a spouse with similar values for his son. Abraham knew it was a great sacrifice sending his servant all the way back to his father's house just to get a wife for his son especially when there were a lot of beautiful Canaanite women all around them. But he also knew that if they paid the price of going to any length to get a wife for his son that shared similar values with them, they would enjoy the benefits tomorrow.

Abraham also learnt from the experience of his nephew, Lot. Lot was a good man who feared God; like Abraham, he also lived among a godless people with godless values. Even though Lot himself lived separate from the vile values of his society, he didn't protect his family from the same. His two daughters where engaged to men from Sodom and his wife's heart was so full of the lifestyle of Sodom, that even when her body left, her heart couldn't.

> *"Meanwhile, the angels questioned Lot. "Do you have any other relatives here in the city?" they asked. "Get them out of this place—your sons-in-law, sons, daughters, or anyone else. For we are about to destroy this city completely. The outcry against this place is so great it has reached the Lord, and he has sent us to destroy it." So Lot rushed out to tell his daughters' fiancés, "Quick, get out of the city! The Lord is about to destroy it." But the young men thought he was only joking. At dawn the next morning the angels became insistent. "Hurry," they said to Lot. "Take your wife and your two daughters who are here. Get out right now, or you will be swept away in the destruction of the city!" When Lot still hesitated, the angels seized his hand and the hands of his wife and two daughters and rushed them to safety outside the city, for the Lord was merciful. When they were safely out of the city, one of the angels ordered, "Run for your lives! And don't look back or stop anywhere in the valley! Escape to the mountains, or you will be swept away!" "Oh no, my lord!" Lot begged. "You have been so gracious to me and saved my life, and you have shown such great kindness. But I cannot go to the mountains. Disaster would catch*

up to me there, and I would soon die. See, there is a small village nearby. Please let me go there instead; don't you see how small it is? Then my life will be saved." "All right," the angel said, "I will grant your request. I will not destroy the little village. But hurry! Escape to it, for I can do nothing until you arrive there." (This explains why that village was known as Zoar, which means "little place.") Lot reached the village just as the sun was rising over the horizon. Then the Lord rained down fire and burning sulfur from the sky on Sodom and Gomorrah. He utterly destroyed them, along with the other cities and villages of the plain, wiping out all the people and every bit of vegetation. But Lot's wife looked back as she was following behind him, and she turned into a pillar of salt.

Genesis 19:12-26 (NLT)

Lot's two daughters' eventually deceived their father to committing incest with them. (Gen 19:30-38).

Abraham knew all this and was determined to protect his son from the evil cultural influence around him. It is very important you marry from your family, by family we mean someone from the same household of faith. It is not enough that you attend the same church or belong to the same group, do you share similar Christian values?

Don't team up with those who are unbelievers. How can righteousness be a partner with wickedness? How can light live with darkness? What harmony can there be between Christ and the devil? How can a believer be a partner with an unbeliever?

2 Corinthians 6:14-15 (NLT)

That you are both believers doesn't mean you share the same Christian values. An unbeliever is not just someone of another faith; it could also be someone with whom you don't share the same core beliefs. If you choose to go into a marriage relationship with someone with whom you have very divergent views in some vital aspect of life, then you can be sure that going ahead with such a relationship is going into trouble because you don't share the same core beliefs.

One thing you must do before you say 'I Do' is ensure yourself and your partner not just share the same faith but all share the same value system, it will spare you unnecessary heart aches.

CHAPTER FOUR

kNoW YouR ROOTS kNoW THE FAMILY YouR INTENDED SPOUSE IS FRoM

"Whose daughter are you?" he asked. "And please tell me, would your father have any room to put us up for the night?" "I am the daughter of Bethuel," she replied. "My grandparents are Nahor and Milcah. Yes, we have plenty of straw and feed for the camels, and we have room for guests."

Genesis 24:23-25 (NLT)

Inasmuch as it is of utmost importance that you marry someone of the same faith and the same core values, it is also important that you know where your intended spouse is coming from. No man is an island, and since you are not Melchizedek, you must have a family you originated from.

You don't just meet someone on the road, or even in church, get into courtship and then and get married without getting the two families or their representatives involved, that is wrong. Even if your intended in laws are of a different faith, you still owe then the honour of letting them know of your plan to marry a member of their family.

Even though Abraham's servant met Rebekah somewhere away from home, he still made enquiries about her family background and made arrangements to meet them. On meeting Rebekah's family, Abraham's servant introduced himself and the family he represented, everything was laid bare and open.

> *"I am Abraham's servant," he explained. "And the Lord has greatly blessed my master; he has become a wealthy man. The Lord has given him flocks of sheep and goats, herds of cattle, a fortune in silver and gold, and many male and female servants and camels and donkeys. "When Sarah, my master's wife, was very old, she gave birth to my master's son, and my master has given him everything he owns. And my master made me take an oath. He said, 'Do not allow my son to marry one of these local Canaanite women. Go instead to my father's house, to my relatives, and find a wife there for my son.'*
>
> **Genesis 24:34-38** (NLT)

You should be very suspicious of someone who claims to love you so much but is not interested in a meeting of your families. Complete openness is a necessity in marriage.

Why is it important you know one another's family background and meet the families?

- It helps you better understand the influences that shaped who you intend to marry.
- It is a sign of honour and respect for the people that gave birth to, brought up and trained the person you intend to marry.
- The families become some sort of accountability system to the intending couple, especially when you all share the similar core values.

Knowing and meeting one another's family is not necessarily allowing external influences control your lives. Getting to know one another's family background is really about getting to understand your intended spouse better and allowing those that matter to you be part of your lives to lend you their support and wealth of experience that can make a world of difference in your marriage.

You don't just meet someone on the road, or even in church, get into courtship, and then and get married without getting your families or representatives involved. That is wrong.

Some, particularly the younger generation believe that there is no need getting the families involve, they say "it's me and my spouse and no one else". This is actually right but it must be within the right context. You shouldn't allow external forces and third party influences control you and your intended spouse but then you also mustn't cut off yourself from positive and enriching relationships that can add value to your family.

There are also times where two intending couple want to marry; they share the same faith and values. They are both from responsible family backgrounds but for no clear reason their families are just opposed to their getting married.

My advice to such parents is that they must know that God hasn't given anyone the power to control the life of another person. We owe it to our children to train them and give them proper guidance but once they are mature enough to marry we must learn to respect their decisions. By all mean parents should express their view about their children's marital choices even if the hold opposing views but they must understand that once their children are grown up and mature enough, their decision should be respected.

If after everything has been said and done in good

faith and the children are still convinced they should marry, the parents should prayerfully support them and commit them to God. To try to force you way on them is manipulation.

The intending couples on their part should do all that is within their power to respectfully and continuously communicate their position to their parents but also realise their marital decision is ultimately theirs.

Before you say "I Do", be sure you know your roots.

CHAPTER FIVE

MENTORING: BEFoRE I Hook up WITH You, I WANT To kNoW WHO YOU LOOK UP TO

"Whose daughter are you?" he asked. "And please tell me, would your father have any room to put us up for the night?" "I am the daughter of Bethuel," she replied. "My grandparents are Nahor and Milcah.

Genesis 24:23-24 (NLT)

The root of a tree is not just the source of the tree; it's also the strength of the tree. Usually, after a heavy rain or a strong wind, some trees will be seen to have fallen because they have been uprooted by the wind; but those with stronger roots remain firm. This implies that the stronger the root of a tree, the more difficult it is for the tree to be uprooted by any external force.

When Abraham's servant met Rebekah, not only did he discover her roots, he also realised the strength of her roots: she was from the same root as his master Abraham was from.

When she heard what Abraham's servant said, she quickly ran home and reported to her family. Rebekah was just meeting Abraham's servant who was a stranger to her; and even more strange were the things he was saying. When she was confronted with such an unusual situation, she quickly ran back to her roots.

> *"Whose daughter are you?" he asked. "And please tell me, would your father have any room to put us up for the night?" "I am the daughter of Bethuel," she replied. "My grandparents are Nahor and Milcah. Yes, we have plenty of straw and feed for the camels, and we have room for guests." The man bowed low and worshiped the Lord. "Praise the Lord, the God of my master, Abraham," he said. "The Lord has shown unfailing love and faithfulness to my master, for he has led me straight to my master's relatives." The young woman ran home to tell her family everything that had happened."*
>
> **Genesis 24:23-28 (NLT)**

Rebekah had people she could run back and report to. Do you? Rebekah had people she was answerable to. Do you?

Before you "hook up" with someone for the rest of your life, it is important you know who that person looks up to. Not only does a tree originate from its root, the root also upholds and sustains the tree.

Closely related to the issue of knowing your root is understanding the power of the root holding you. Just like the tree hold the root. There must be people that hold you, people you hold yourself accountable to, people that you look up to as models and mentors.

It is dangerous to marry someone who has no mentor!

- Your mentor is your teacher,
- Your mentor is your trainer

- Your mentor is a picture of your future
- Your mentor has a roadmap to your future.
- Your mentor challenges you to be better.
- Your mentor corrects you and calls you to order whenever you err.
- Your mentor may or may not be your parents.
- Your mentor may or may not be older than you.

One of the scriptural reasons for parenting is *Mentoring*, but many parents do not understand this, so they don't make conscious efforts to provide effective mentoring for their children.

Never marry someone that is not accountable to anyone. You must always have people around you that can call you to order no matter who you are. As great as Moses was, and with the privilege of having God speak to him face to face, Jethro his father in-law was still able to correct him.

> *"Moses listened to his father-in-law's advice and followed his suggestions."*
>
> **Exodus 18:24 (NLT)**

Every power device has a control mechanism; the purpose of the control mechanism is to regulate the operation of the device so that it can work maximally without being hazardous to the user. Everyone must have relationships that can help regulate their conduct.

When you see a person who does not have such relationships but still insist on going into a marriage relationship with the person, then you can be sure you are heading for trouble. You are dancing with the devil and he'll surely make a fool of you.

A person who has nobody that can call him or her to order is like a car without brakes, its crash is imminent, it's just a matter of time. If you want to marry someone, and all the person does is take you out to places you enjoy and not to

A person who has nobody that can call him or her to order is like a car without brakes. Its crash is imminent; it's just a matter of time.

people they are accountable to, run away fast!

Tell the person you want to marry "I will like to meet the people you are accountable to." If the person says "I am accountable only to God and not any man..." discuss with the person the importance of a mentoring relationship and encourage the person to get one. If the person insists on not needing anyone to be accountable to but God, break the relationship and wish the person well.

Your mentors shouldn't just be people you relate with and follow by books and electronic media, you must also have mentors you can sit face to face with and ask questions.

When, Abraham's servant met Rebekah, it wasn't just her beauty and attitude that was captivating; it was also, her roots. And this was not just because he knew them, but also because Rebekah had shown herself accountable to them. Rebekah and her family were also comfortable with Isaac because it was clear he was accountable to his father, Abraham.

Never marry someone that is not accountable to anyone.

Please understand that your mentors are not meant to control or manipulate your life; they are there simply to guide you.

Before you hook up with anyone in marriage for the rest of your life be sure you know the people they look up to. If you are already in a relationship and you don't have a mentor you both meet with, prayerfully consider choosing a person or some people, and make yourself accountable to them. This one of the things you must do before you say "I Do".

CHAPTER SIX

MAN, IF You LOVE HER GO AFTER HER

"Go instead to my homeland, to my relatives, and find a wife there for my son Isaac."

Genesis 24:4 (NLT)

God created man to be an initiator, to be a finder, to be a seeker, particularly as it concerns marriage. Abraham, representing Isaac initiated the move for marriage. Even after Isaac and Rebekah eventually met, it was Isaac that made the move to bring in Rebekah.

"And Isaac brought Rebekah into his mother Sarah's tent, and she became his wife. He loved her deeply, and she was a special comfort to him after the death of his mother."

Genesis 24:67 (NLT)

As the one who is to head the home under God, it is important that the man begins to show the qualities of great leadership by being the initiator of the relationship. If you want to marry, then begin to initiate the process. If there is a lady you love and desire to marry, then make the first move and let her know. This might come easier for some guys than others, but however it maybe, it usually best that the man initiates the process.

> *"The man who finds a wife finds a treasure, and he receives favor from the Lord."*
>
> **Proverbs 18:22 (NLT)**

It says "The man who finds a wife..." Abraham's servant left his home, his comfort zone and travelled far to find a wife for his master's son.

How far are you willing to go to find the lady you love?

Are you willing to go beyond your comfort zone for her?

Yes, you are an introvert and a shy man but can you break these seeming limitations for the woman you love? The extent a man goes in his pursuit of the lady he loves, particularly when he is doing it without ulterior motives give an idea how he will treasure her as a wife. Love must have evidence. John said:

> *"Dear children, let us not love with words or tongue but with actions and in truth."*
>
> **1 John 3:18 (NIV)**

If he can't show he loves you by initiating a move for marriage or initiating a healthy discussion on the future of your relationship, then you as a lady should be very careful proceeding into marriage with him.

I know in some cases, some ladies believe they must play unrealistically "hard to get". They believe if they don't play hard to get, the prospective suitor might not value them.

The truth is that your value doesn't come from what you do; your value is in who you are. A lady shouldn't cheapen herself but that doesn't mean you should make yourself difficult to be found.

To get Adam a wife cost him a rib, but didn't cause him pain. It shouldn't cause a man pain to find a wife. If it's painful finding a wife, then what will it take to live with that wife! Adam was the one to initiate discussions with Eve, but she was accessible and "findable".

> *"So the Lord God caused the man to fall into a deep sleep. While the man slept, the Lord God took out one of the man's ribs and closed up the opening. Then the Lord God made a woman from the rib, and he brought her to the man. "At last!" the man exclaimed. "This one is bone from my bone, and flesh from my flesh! She will be called 'woman,' because she was taken from 'man."*
>
> **Genesis 2:21-23 (NLT)**

The extent a man goes in his pursuit of the lady he loves, particularly when he is doing it without ulterior motives give an idea how he will treasure her as a wife. Love must have evidence.

Boaz was the one that initiated marriage arrangement with Ruth, but she was accessible and "findable". (Ruth 3). A man who will lead a home must start taking some lead before getting married. If he not willing to take leadership and initiate the process of marriage, don't force it on him. This is a major quality you must look out for before you say "I DO"

CHAPTER SEVEN

LADY, IF You cANT FOLLOW HIM ALL THE WAY DON'T FOLLOW HIM AT ALL

"Well," they said, "we'll call Rebekah and ask her what she thinks." So they called Rebekah. "Are you willing to go with this man?" they asked her. And she replied, "Yes, I will go." So they said good-bye to Rebekah and sent her away with Abraham's servant..."

Genesis 24:57-59 (NLT)

To think marriage will not change you is self-deception; it will. Whether it will make you better or worse is up to you; but you can be certain that marriage will never leave you the same.

One of the causes of marital crises is lack of understanding of the biblical demands of marriage. While the Bible obligates that a man provides leadership for his family, it also obligates the woman to follow the leadership of her husband.

A woman who doesn't understand this demand or is unwillingly to be committed to it is not ready for a good marriage. Why should you commit to marrying a man when you cannot submit to his leadership?

Rebekah was asked if she was willing to leave all she had to follow, her husband to be, Isaac, she said "Yes". That was a huge step and it shows the level maturity and clarity of mind that marriage requires. The feeling of love and "chemistry" is good but it takes much more than that to have a good marriage. You need to understand what you are getting into.

A wife is meant to be a helper, but how can you be a helper to a man you have not committed to following all the way, and for the rest of your life.

If you choose to marry a man, then you are marrying him in totality, accommodating his strengths, weaknesses, and all.

Don't marry a man whom you don't believe in.

Don't marry a man you are ashamed of.

Don't marry a man believing you will change him once you get married.

If you cannot accept him in totality for what he is now, and also be willing to live with him that way for the rest of your life, then you need to put your marriage arrangements on hold until you are sure.

Nobody has the power to truly change anyone. People change because they choose to change. Marrying a man whom you have not resolved in your heart to follow all the way, but hoping that you will change him is setting yourself up for marital frustrations.

Abigail was a very good woman, but for some reason she was married to a very foolish man called Nabal. She accepted her position as the wise wife of a foolish man and used her wisdom to protect and cover her husband's foolishness; she didn't expose it.

When her husband offended David and Abigail heard about it, she didn't bother abusing or arguing with Nabal for the trouble he had caused, she simply, in her wisdom, took action to resolve the situation.

When Abigail saw David, she quickly got off her donkey and bowed low before him. She fell at his feet and said, "I accept all blame in this matter, my lord. Please listen to what I have to say. I know Nabal is a wicked and ill-tempered man; please don't pay any attention to him. He is a fool, just as his name suggests. But I never even saw the young men you sent. "Now, my lord, as surely as the Lord lives and you yourself live, since the Lord has kept you from murdering and taking vengeance into your own hands, let all your enemies and those who try to harm you be as cursed as Nabal is. And here is a present that I, your servant, have brought to you and your young men. Please forgive me if I have offended you in any way. The Lord will surely reward you with a lasting dynasty, for you are fighting the Lord's battles. And you have not done wrong throughout your entire life. "Even when you are chased by those who seek to kill you, your life is safe in the care of the Lord your God, secure in his treasure pouch! But the lives of your enemies will disappear like stones shot from a sling! When the Lord has done all he promised and has made you leader of Israel, don't let this be a blemish on your record. Then your conscience won't have to bear the staggering burden of needless bloodshed and vengeance. And when the Lord has done these great things for you, please remember me, your servant!" David replied to Abigail, "Praise the Lord, the God of Israel, who has sent you to meet me today! Thank God for your good sense! Bless you for keeping me from murder and from carrying out vengeance with my own hands. For I swear by the Lord, the God of Israel, who has kept me from hurting you, that if you had not hurried out to meet me, not one of

1 Samuel 25:23-35 (NLT)

Nabal's men would still be alive tomorrow morning." Then David accepted her present and told her, "Return home in peace. I have heard what you said. We will not kill your husband."

Don't marry a man believing you will change him once you get married.

Abigail knew that in marrying Nabal, a fool, she had become "Mrs. Fool". In marrying a foolish man like Nabal, she had committed to following him all the way. Nabal had a public testimony of foolishness that even his staff knew about and Abigail also had a public testimony of being a wise and understanding wife. She never used his foolishness against him; she knew that solution wasn't in trying to change him or constantly argue with him. She simply remained a committed wife and used her wisdom to protect her husband and her household.

Doing this for years must have been very challenging for Abigail, but God has a way of helping those that do things His way. A woman like Abigail is a priceless treasure any day. There is no right thinking man that will not want such a woman as a wife. The moment David heard that Nabal was dead he immediately made a marriage proposal to Abigail.

When David heard that Nabal was dead, he said, "Praise the Lord, who has avenged the insult I received from Nabal and has kept me from doing it myself. Nabal has received the punishment for his sin." Then David sent messengers to Abigail to ask her to become his wife.

1 Samuel 25:39 (NLT)

Abigail knew that in marrying Nabal, she had to follow him all the way, no matter what.

Lady, before you marry, understands that your

"cards" are in your hands and you can play them however you wish. Don't, due to some pressure, commit to a marriage today that you will regret tomorrow.

Ask the man all the questions you need to ask him and ask yourself if you can live with him as his helper and not as his leader for the rest of your life. If you are not completely sure you can do this, please don't say "I DO".

CHAPTER EIGHT

pRopER PHYSICAL pREpARATIoN

"So the servant took an oath by putting his hand under the thigh of his master, Abraham. He swore to follow Abraham's instructions. Then he loaded ten of Abraham's camels with all kinds of expensive gifts from his master, and he traveled to distant Aram-naharaim. There he went to the town where Abraham's brother Nahor had settled. He made the camels kneel beside a well just outside the town. It was evening, and the women were coming out to draw water.

Genesis 24:9-11 (NLT)

Getting a wife for Isaac was a very serious issue. Abraham understood the huge responsibility God had placed upon him and his family, so he was determined to make sure things didn't go wrong in his lineage. After settling the spiritual aspect of things, they also ensured they made adequate physical preparation too. Abraham had ensured he followed what God had laid out for him in the covenant, they also prayed and committed the matter to God, thereby settling the spiritual side. Now they had to balance the matter by putting the physical preparation in place.

Sometime, Christians make very thorough and extensive spiritual preparation but very poor physical preparation. We are not just spiritual beings, we are also physical beings. Most people will actually relate with us first on a physical level before they get to relate with us on a spiritual level.

Abraham knew he was a blessed man and that the blessing was going to pass on to Isaac, but he also understood that the blessing wasn't a physical thing. When his servant was going to get Isaac a wife, Abraham didn't just send them with the intangible blessing alone, they also prepared physically and went with tangible thing to show the intended bride and her family.

Many single people have prayed, fasted and done all sorts and have received clear words from God about their marital future, but instead of taking action based on what they have received, they claim they are "waiting on God". There is a place for waiting on God, but there are also a number of physical steps that need to be taken in preparation for marriage.

Abraham's servant had to prepare to leave where he was, go out of their comfort area in Canaan and travel to Mesopotamia to meet Isaac's spouse. He also took a lot of gifts to give the intended bride and her family. We must never discard or underrate the place of physical preparation and physical things.

After all that Rebekah heard, she ran home and told her family and showed them the jewelleries she was given as a proof of her story.

"The young woman ran home to tell her family everything that had happened. Now Rebekah had a brother named Laban, who ran out to meet the man at the spring. He had seen the nose-ring and the bracelets on his sister's wrists, and had heard Rebekah tell what the man had said. So he rushed out to the spring, where the man was still standing beside his camels. Laban said to him, "Come and stay with us, you who are blessed by the Lord! Why are you standing here outside the town when I have a room all ready for you and a place prepared for the camels?"

Genesis 24:28-31 (NLT)

Laban, Rebekah's brother had run out to meet Abraham's servant because of the gifts he saw with his sister and not just the things she said. In the physical world, physical things are very important. Proverbs 18:16 helps us understand that gifts will help get people's attention.

"A gift gets attention; it buys the attention of eminent people."

Proverbs 18:16 (MSG)

Physical preparation goes beyond material possession and gift presentation, it also includes issues like knowing your physical health condition. Knowing one another's family background, financial situation, educational or health status is part of physical preparation. To demand to know your future partner's genotype, blood group etc is not a sign of carnality. Marriage is not just about sharing your life together spiritually, you will certainly share your life together physically too.

Physical preparation is not all there is to getting

married, but it is important aspect nonetheless. So before you say "I do" ensure you make adequate physical preparation.

CHAPTER NINE

I kNoW You'RE PRAYING buT bE SuRE You;RE WATCHING

"When she had given him a drink, she said, "I'll draw water for your camels, too, until they have had enough to drink." So she quickly emptied her jug into the watering trough and ran back to the well to draw water for all his camels. The servant watched her in silence, wondering whether or not the Lord had given him success in his mission."

Genesis 24:19-21 (NLT)

Some believe that love is blind, but that is not true. Love actually sees and sees very well. After you might have closed your eyes in prayers for your marriage partner, ensure you open your eyes well and watch!

Jesus told His disciples in the Garden of Gethsemane "...watch and pray so that you do not fall..." Matt 26:41. Many have fallen into to unimaginable heartaches because they were not watching.

The bible says Abraham's servant watched Rebekah

closely, wondering. He was not just watching and basking in Rebekah's beauty; he was wondering and asking questions within himself.

When you marry, you marry a person in their entirety. You don't take the body and the behaviour is left behind; so, when deciding whom to marry, you must watch closely the spiritual, emotional, mental and physical qualities. What kind of family heritage does the person have; you need to watch all these things.

After the prayer meeting and spiritual strategy session that Abraham and his servant had about a spouse for his child, Abraham was still very particular about the family heritage of his to be in-laws. He said "based on what I have seen of the Canaanite women around here, on no account should my son pick a wife from these people. But travel back to my home country, I know the people there; pick a wife for my son from there."

> *"One day Abraham said to his oldest servant, the man in charge of his household:"Take an oath by putting your hand under my thigh. Swear by the Lord, the God of heaven and earth, that you will not allow my son to marry one of these local Canaanite women. Go instead to my homeland, to my relatives, and find a wife there for my son Isaac."*

Genesis 24:2-4 (NLT)

Abraham also told his servant to look out for the attitude of the lady, he said if she has an unwilling attitude with respect with following you back here, don't bother considering her for my son.

If she is unwilling to come back with you, then you are free from this oath of mine. But under no circumstances are you to take my son there." **Genesis 24:8 (NLT)**

So after all the prayer, Abraham's servant knew he had to watch out keenly for a woman from Abraham's father's house and he had to watch out for the woman's attitude, she must have a willing attitude with respect to joining Isaac where he was.

Another thing you must watch out for is looks. Remember you are also a physical human being; you must like what you see. Obviously looks are not the most important criteria for choosing a life partner. Proverbs 31:30 says, *Charm can be deceptive and beauty doesn't last, but a woman who fears and reverences God shall be greatly praised.* (TLB). But this doesn't imply that looks are unimportant All the patriarchs had beautiful wives.

Abraham: *But as he was approaching the borders of Egypt, he asked Sarai his wife to tell everyone that she was his sister! "You are very beautiful," he told her, "and when the Egyptians see you they will say, 'This is his wife. Let's kill him and then we can have her!' But if you say you are my sister, then the Egyptians will treat me well because of you, and spare my life!" And sure enough, when they arrived in Egypt everyone spoke of her beauty.* **Genesis 12:11-14** (TLB)

Isaac: *As he was still speaking to the Lord about this, a beautiful young girl named Rebekah arrived with a water jug on her shoulder and filled it at the spring. (Her father was Bethuel the son of Nahor and his wife Milcah.)* Genesis 24:15-16 (TLB)

The men of the place questioned him about his wife. He said, "She's my sister." He was afraid to say "She's my wife." He was thinking, "These men might kill me to get Rebekah, she's so beautiful." Genesis 26:7 (MSG)

kEEp IT TOGETHER No MATTER HoW TOUGH

Rebekah was very beautiful and old enough to be married, but she was still a virgin...

Genesis 24:16 (NLT)

Sexual desire is something that God has put naturally in every man. The desire for sex is not from the devil as some believe; it is from the Holy and all wise God. God gave mankind the gift of sex for the purposes of procreation and pleasure. But just like every gift that God gives, the devil found a way of perverting it.

The abuse of certain things do not necessary mean those things are bad in themselves. Electricity has been used by some people to torture others and kill them but that doesn't mean electricity is not useful, nor does it cancel its original purpose.

Just because some people abuse sex doesn't mean we should forget and lose its original God-intended purpose.

God designed sex to be experienced within the confines of marriage; any other use of sex is an abuse. Just like it is an offense to drive a car without a driver's license, it is an offense to practice sex without license. And the sex license is only given after you take your marriage vow.

Even though Rebekah was very beautiful and of marriageable age, she was still a virgin when she met her husband.

Virginity is nobility.
Virginity is a virtue.

Just because some people because some people abuse sex doesn't mean it we should forget and lose its original God-intended purpose.

Under the Law of Moses, a woman that was not a virgin before marriage was put to death because it was a disgrace to be sexually active outside marriage. (see Deuteronomy 22:13-21).

Today a lot of people jump in and out of bed with all sorts of people with absolutely no consideration of their virginity. In our society today many believe it is a thing of shame to be a virgin when going into marriage, you are consider old fashioned and unexposed even by some who profess the Christian faith!

Paul, writing to the church at Ephesus, said, *"Let there be no sex sin, impurity or greed among you. Let no one be able to accuse you of any such things."* **Ephesians 5:3** (TLB)

The truth is that with the level of sexual perversion that flows freely in our society, even in broad daylight, it is tough taking a stand for sexual purity but it is not impossible. The bible says in Job 31:1 *"I made a solemn pact with myself never to undress a girl with my eyes* (MSG)

It is important we keep our sexual drive under control until we are married. 2 Timothy 1:7 says, *For God did not give us a spirit of timidity, but a spirit of power, of love and of self-discipline.* (NIV)

So we have the God-given ability for self-discipline and self-control. Trust in God's grace to keep you sexually pure until you get married.

If you are already sexually active before marriage, you must understand that God still loves you. Don't condemn yourself or allow yourself wallow in guilt and despair. The blood of Jesus makes us brand new people in Christ. Ask God for forgiveness, stop engaging in pre- marital sex and walk in sexual purity as Christ's chaste virgin cleansed by His blood.

Keeping your virginity is something you must do before you say "I DO"

Virginity is nobility.

Virginity is a virtue.

CHAPTER ELEVEN

IF You'RE NoT READY To LEAVE DoN'T TRY To CLEAVE!

So they called Rebekah. "Are you willing to go with this man?" they asked her. And she replied, "Yes, I will go." So they said good-bye to Rebekah and sent her away with Abraham's servant and his men. The woman who had been Rebekah's childhood nurse went along with her. They gave her this blessing as she parted..."

Genesis 24:58-60 (NLT)

When a man and a woman decide to get married, it means they have decided to place their relationship above every other human relationship. It means they are deciding to forsake all other human relationship and become one in marriage. This is a very huge decision, and the process of forsaking all others to become one with your spouse, making your spouse the priority relationship in your life is not a very easy one.

How easy is it to meet a person for a few months or even years and decide that I am willing to make the relationship with this person the priority relationship of my life? Valuing this relationship above that of my parents and siblings I have know all my life, above relationships with childhood friends etc. If you think deeply about it, it's a tough decision but that is the decision you have to make if you have decided to get married.

While presiding over the first marriage on earth, God made this statement.

"For this reason a man will leave his father and mother and be united to his wife, and they will become one flesh."

Genesis 2:24(NIV)

Marriage is the reason a man and a woman will leave the longest relationship in their lives; the relationship with their parents; and be joined as one with their spouse. This leaving is a very challenging process both physically and emotionally but particularly emotionally. Jesus re-echoed the same position on marriage thousands of years later when He said, *"...For this cause shall a man leave father and mother, and shall cleave to his wife..."* {Matthew 19:5 (KJV)}

To cleave is an old English word that means to join together or glue together. So, before you claim you are ready to be joined with your partner in marriage, are you willing to leave physically and emotionally?

Many marriages are in trouble today because of third party influences. Third party influences are human relationships outside that of the husband and wife that exert greater influence on the marriage than the husband and wife. One major reason for that is, the couple involved didn't fully leave all other relationships, and so cleaving in marriage became a major problem.

Leaving doesn't begin in marriage, you must begin the process of both physical and emotional disengagement as you begin to grow up and mature.

Ecclesiastes 3:1 says: *" To everything there is a season, A time for every purpose under heaven."*

There is a time to cleave to your parents, siblings and close friend, in fact these relationship usually form the inner circle of people you confide in before deciding who to marry. But the moment you have decided on whom to marry; a process of role reversal begins where the person you decide to marry becomes THE INNER CIRCLE and those who were in the inner circle take their places behind your spouse.

When a man and a woman decide to get married, it means they have decided to place their relationship above every other human relationship.

If you are not ready to make this adjustment particularly emotionally then you can be sure you are not ready to be happily married.

Rebekah's family members asked her if she was willing to leave her family and cleave to Isaac and her answer was – Yes. After her consent, her family bid her farewell and she departed. Without that departure their marriage would not have had a future.

When a woman is pregnant with a child, the umbilical cord connects the mother and the child together till the child is born. While in the womb, the baby's life is dependent on being connected to the mother by the umbilical cord. But after the baby is born, the same cord that was necessary for the baby's survival is no longer necessary; the baby has to be detached from the umbilical cord. If the cord is not cut off, that which at a time was necessary for the baby's life can now become the cause of the baby's death.

If you do not see a wiliness on the part of you fiancé or fiancée to leave the father and mother then you can be sure you are not ready for marriage, especially a happy one. A person who cannot make a decision in courtship except daddy and mummy knows about it is not ready to leave and therefore cannot properly cleave. A man that believes that he can be planning to marry and still want to be hanging out with the boys and the babes as he used to is certainly not ready for marriage and the same goes for the woman.

There is a huge difference between courtship and marriage and that difference is deeper commitment. With deeper commitment comes greater responsibility to your intended spouse. The lady that is preparing for marriage but is more interested in how to keep up with the latest fashion trends than learning to keep a home is certainly not ready to leave the lifestyle of a single lady and cleave to the demands of a married woman.

Earlier we had discussed the virtues of virginity before marriage. Sex before marriage is another thing that can make it difficult cleaving with your spouse in marriage.

Sex is what consummates the marriage covenant and covenants have implications that transcend the physical. God designed sex to be only with your marriage partner, because sex joins you both physically and spiritually with the person you engage in sex with. 1 Corinthians 6:16 says:

And don't you know that if a man joins himself to a prostitute she becomes a part of him and he becomes a part of her? For God tells us in the Scripture that in his sight the two become one person. (TLB)

The message translation renders it this way, 1 Corinthians 6:16 (MSG)

There's more to sex than mere skin on skin. Sex is as much spiritual mystery as physical fact. As written in Scripture, "The two become one."

So in summary, sex joins you with the person you have sexual relationships with. So how can you properly join with your spouse when you have been joined with someone else through pre- marital sex? Also in line with this is the sin of pornography. Jesus said:

"But I tell you that anyone who looks at a woman lustfully has already committed adultery with her in his heart."

Matthew 5:28 (NIV)

The message translation says,

But don't think you've preserved your virtue simply by staying out of bed. Your heart can be corrupted by lust even quicker than your body. Those leering looks you think nobody notices—they also corrupt.

Matthew 5:28 (MSG)

Leaving all others does not begin after you say I DO, it begins long before then. When you say "I DO" you should have be completely detached from all others so you can properly cleave to your spouse. This is something you must do before you say" I DO".

CHAPTER TWELVE

A HOME To LIVE AND MAKE A LIVING

Meanwhile, Isaac, whose home was in the Negev, had returned from Beer-lahai-roi. One evening as he was walking and meditating in the fields, he looked up and saw the camels coming. When Rebekah looked up and saw Isaac, she quickly dismounted from her camel. "Who is that man walking through the fields to meet us?" she asked the servant. And he replied, "It is my master." So Rebekah covered her face with her veil. Then the servant told Isaac everything he had done. And Isaac brought Rebekah into his mother Sarah's tent, and she became his wife. He loved her deeply, and she was a special comfort to him after the death of his mother.

Genesis 24:62-67 (NLT)

A place to live is an essential part of the journey to marriage. After leaving your father and mother, you will need a place to live. Before Adam got a wife, he got a home – the Garden of Eden. Jesus said foxes raise their families in holes and birds raise their families in nest (Luk 9:58). You too will need a home to live and raise your family.

The society back in those days was more closely knit and communal than it is today. It wasn't unusual then for fathers to provide a place to live for their sons getting married. The place was usually a room in the main house or a building in a section of the family compound. The bible says in Deuteronomy 24:5, "*When a man takes a new wife, he is not to go out with the army or be given any business or work duties. He gets one year off simply to be at home making his wife happy.* (MSG)

The communal way they lived made this possible; people within the extended family system will ensure the new couple are taken care of properly within that one year. If you try that today, yourself and your spouse might starve except you have a very strong financial reserve!

When you are in that age range where you begin to seriously consider marriage ensure your relationships with the opposite sex are very well defined.

The society is different today, in the sense that you might not have someone to provide a place for you to live but you need a place to live, and it is necessary you ensure it is available. This is usually the responsibility of the man as the head of the home. But there is nothing wrong in the intending couple to jointly work toward ensuring they have a place to live once they are married.

After Rebekah's long journey from her father's house, her new home was her husband's house. Isaac had his home in the Negev, it's important you have your own home too. It doesn't have to be the one you built personally; it's not about how expensive it is. It is just meant to be a simple, safe and decent place for you to begin to build your own new family.

Again, because the housing challenges of modern society, it is important intending couples are mindful of this fact as early as possible and begin prayerfully and practically preparing for it.

The place Isaac and Rebekah live was a place where they brought themselves comfort. Some people make the mistake thinking it is the place you live that gives you comfort and peace. No doubt this can be true, but what really make a home are the people living in it not the place in itself. So don't just put emphasis on the place, be the kind of couple that can make a little corner look great, full of love and warmth.

The home is not just a place to sleep, wake up and receive guests. It is your place of raising a new generation and moulding destinies. It is the place where you shape values and live out the values of a new lineage you are raising in the midst of others.

So get a place you can call your home. With every other thing in place, having your own home will surely make it easier for you to say "I DO".

CHAPTER THIRTEEN

LET THE OFFER bE CLEAR oN THE OFFER

Then food was served. But Abraham's servant said, "I don't want to eat until I have told you why I have come." "All right," Laban said, "tell us." "I am Abraham's servant," he explained. "And the Lord has greatly blessed my master; he has become a wealthy man. The Lord has given him flocks of sheep and goats, herds of cattle, a fortune in silver and gold, and many male and female servants and camels and donkeys."When Sarah, my master's wife, was very old, she gave birth to my master's son, and my master has given him everything he owns. And my master made me take an oath. He said, 'Do not allow my son to marry one of these local Canaanite women. Go instead to my father's house, to my relatives, and find a wife there for my son.'

Genesis 24:33-38 (NLT)

Marriage is a covenant, this fact cannot be overemphasized. No one goes into covenants without having a clear idea of what he or she is getting into. People that go into covenants

No one goes into covenants without having a clear idea of what he or she is getting into.

based on assumptions usually have themselves to blame.

In the book of Joshua 9:3-18, the Gibeonites came to the Israeli camp and deceived them into making a covenant. They showed the leaders of Israel their worn out wine skin and dry bread and based on that Israel assumed they travelled from a very far country not realising they were their neighbours.

This assumption cost Israel a lot because they had to live with the Gibeonites peacefully. God even punished Israel when Saul killed some Gibeonites.

> *There was a famine during David's reign that lasted for three years, so David asked the Lord about it. And the Lord said, "The famine has come because Saul and his family are guilty of murdering the Gibeonites."*
>
> **Samuel 21:1** (NLT)

One of the problem areas for single people is the marriage proposal. There are many that have assumed that they were in a relationship leading to marriage when in reality there was no such thing. Some have assumed that a good friendship relationship with the opposite sex was a courtship when in reality it is simply a close friendship. When people are in relationships with this kind of assumption, they have set themselves up for frustrations and heart aches.

When you are in that age range where you begin to seriously consider marriage ensure your relationships with the opposite sex are very well defined. Friendship is not courtship and courtship is not marriage. Friendship could lead to courtship and courtship could lead to marriage but they are not all the same.

Marriage is not a joke; it is a serious human institution. If you are taking your relationship into marriage it must be very clear and a proper proposal is in order.

A proper proposal is not necessarily a ceremony where you call people together, present a ring or make some elaborate preparation around it and there is nothing wrong doing any of that too. By proper marriage proposal, I mean a time when a clear and serious marriage request is made known to the person you intend to marry and there is a **clear and unmistakable** response from the person.

After a long and tiring journey, Laban brought Abraham's servant into the family house and was going to begin entertainment. Abraham's servant however refused the entertainment. He was already in Abraham's family house, he had seen Rebekah. The prayer condition he had secretly prayed to God was already met by Rebekah; she had even received the jewelleries he gave her. What else did he want? He wanted to formally make a marriage proposal for Rebekah on Isaac's behalf and also get the response. This proposal and response was so important to him that he wouldn't even consider the customary entertainment appropriate until that was settled.

If you are serious about your relationships and you one day want to settle into marriage, learn to define the purpose of every relationship you are involved in especially relationships with the opposite sex.

Don't assume a marriage proposal or a response when there is none. Remember, marriage is a covenant, ensure you get into it properly. A proposal and response is just appropriate. **This is something you must do before you say "I DO."**

CHAPTER FOURTEEN

SAY 'I DO'

"So they called Rebekah. "Are you willing to go with this man?" they asked her. And she replied, "Yes, I will go." So they said good-bye to Rebekah and sent her away with Abraham's servant and his men. The woman who had been Rebekah's childhood nurse went along with her."

Genesis 24:58-59 (NLT)

I DO" is the affirmative consent that the parties involved in a marriage ceremony must give if the ceremony is to be called successful.

When the minister asks, "Who gives this woman in marriage?"

The bride's father answers, "I DO"

Then the minister as the groom, "Do you take this woman... as your lawfully wedded wife?"

The groom then answers, **"I DO."**

The minister asks the bride also, "Do you take this man... as your lawfully wedded husband?"

The bride also answers, **"I DO."**

After these series of affirmative answers and some other things, the minister then finally says, **"Now I declare you man and wife"**

The proposal is never the end of the journey; it's simply the beginning of another phase in the journey to marriage. After the proposal, you must perform the ultimate purpose of the proposal—the wedding.

Somewhere in the course of the wedding ceremony, the person administering the vows will demand you affirm you commitment to your spouse to be in the presence of witnesses. "I DO" is what represents this affirmation.

"I DO" means you are going into the marriage without coercion.
"I DO" means you are going ahead with the marriage of your own volition with your full consent.
"I DO" means you have counted the cost and you understand the demands of the decision you are making and are still willing to go ahead into the marriage.
"I DO." These two words will change your life forever.

Because of the life changing impact these words will have on your life, the minister usually will structure the wedding vows to ensure you say "I DO" several times.

After the proposal and all the eating and drinking at Bethuel's house, the time came to ask Rebekah about her wishes; after all, she would be the one to live with Isaac. When they asked if she was willing to go and join her future husband, her answer was **"Yes, I will go."** It was an affirmative answer, her own form of **"I DO"**

You should only say "I DO" when you are sure it is to a future of peace, trust, understanding, and love. You should say "I DO" when you are convinced it is with the person you truly love and who loves you truly—a person with whom you share mutual respect.

Remember, when you say "I DO" it will never leave you the same. For some people, saying "I DO" has been one of the best things that they did in their lives. For some others, saying "I DO" has been the worst mistake of their life.

I am praying for you that your decision to say "I DO" will usher you into a blessed and fulfilling marriage filled with godly seeds and the fulfilment of godly dreams

Keep all these 14 points close to your heart; they are things you must ensure you are mindful of and commit yourself to before you say "I DO"

SoMETHING IMPORTANT THAT You MUST ALSo DO

Sometime we know we need to make some changes in our lives but we don't seem to find the strength within ourselves to do it. God wants to empower you with the grace to do the things you need to do. That grace has already been made available in Christ. Paul the Apostle said in Philippians 4:13, *"For I can do everything through Christ, who gives me strength."* The way to connect to the "can do" strength in Christ begins with relationship with Him. If you want Jesus in your life to empower you with that ability to do the things you need to do, please say this prayer:

Father, I come to you now in the name of Jesus and I ask that you forgive me. Come into my heart, be my Saviour and Lord, help me experience that Comeback Grace as I came back to you today. In Jesus' Name I have prayed.

Congratulations! We would love to hear the story of what God is doing in your life through this book. Please contact us to share your story with us:
T: +234 805 7200 197, +234 808 785 4854, +234 702 528 7000
E: sandc.tools@gmail.com

THE BOOK

Very few decisions have the power to affect your life as much as deciding on the person you choose to spend the rest of your life with.

- **Your choice of school**
- **Your choice of work**
- **The place you live**

No other decision demands your entire life in exchange. Even when you join the military, once you retire, you are free to return to civil life. But for marriage, it's

"...till death do us part..."

Once you say "I DO", you are in; but how many people really go into marriage knowing what they are doing when they say "I DO"? How have they been properly prepared to know the kind of person to say "I DO" to? How many people know the things you need to look out for before saying "I DO"?

The purpose of this book is to give you a scriptural guide on what to do before you commit your life to saying "I DO" to anyone. Whether you are single or married, this book will be of great help to you and to someone you love.

Adeniyi Adekunle

adeNiyi Adekunle is called of God to communicate scriptural principles to impact man and influence culture. He serves as the pastor of The Strong Nation Ministries and President of Light for Living International, a ministry committed to teaching and training believers on how to enrich their lives and relationships through the finished work of Christ and how to influence their societies by living out biblical values. He is a graduate of Electronics/ Telecommunications Engineering and is currently completing his thesis for a Master's degree in Leadership.Adeniyi is happily married with two lovely daughters.

www.ingramcontent.com/pod-product-compliance
Lightning Source LLC
LaVergne TN
LVHW040913150826
845672LV00007B/2028

* 9 7 8 9 7 8 9 4 2 9 5 5 4 *